BASKETBALL LEGENDS

Kareem Abdul-Jabbar
Charles Barkley
Larry Bird
Wilt Chamberlain
Clyde Drexler
Julius Erving
Patrick Ewing
Anfernee Hardaway
The Head Coaches
Grant Hill
Juwan Howard
Allen Iverson
Magic Johnson
Michael Jordan
Shawn Kemp
Jason Kidd
Reggie Miller
Alonzo Mourning
Hakeem Olajuwon
Shaquille O'Neal
Gary Payton
Scottie Pippen
David Robinson
Dennis Rodman
John Stockton

CHELSEA HOUSE PUBLISHERS

JOHN STOCKTON

John Wukovits

Introduction by
Chuck Daly

CHELSEA HOUSE PUBLISHERS
Philadelphia

Produced by Duke & Company
Devon, Pennsylvania

Picture Research: Sandy Jones
Cover Illustration: Bradford Brown

First Printing

1 3 5 7 9 8 6 4 2

Library of Congress Cataloging-in-Publication Data

Wukovits, John F., 1944–
John Stockton / by John Wukovits.
p.   cm.—(Basketball legends)
Includes bibliographical references (p.) and index.
Summary: Presents a biography of the Utah Jazz point guard who holds the
NBA record for most career assists.
ISBN 0-7910-4579-X
1. Stockton, John, 1962—Juvenile literature.   2. Basketball players—United
States—Biography—Juvenile literature.   3. Utah Jazz (Basketball team)—
Juvenile literature. [1. Stockton, John, 1962–.   2. Basketball players.]   I. Title.
II. Series.
GV884.S76W84   1998
796.323'092—dc21
[B]   97-50120
                                                                              CIP
                                                                              AC

CONTENTS

BECOMING A
BASKETBALL LEGEND

Chuck Daly

What does it take to be a basketball superstar? Two of the three things it takes are easy to spot. Any great athlete must have excellent skills and tremendous dedication. The third quality needed is much harder to define, or even put in words. Others call it leadership or desire to win, but I'm not sure that explains it fully. This third quality relates to the athlete's thinking process, a certain mentality and work ethic. One can coach athletic skills, and while few superstars need outside influence to help keep them dedicated, it is possible for a coach to offer some well-timed words in order to keep that athlete fully motivated. But a coach can do no more than appeal to a player's will to win; how much that player is then capable of ensuring victory is up to his own internal workings.

In recent times, we have been fortunate to have seen some of the best to play the game. Larry Bird, Magic Johnson, and Michael Jordan had all three components of superstardom in full measure. They brought their teams to numerous championships, and made the players around them better. (They also made their coaches look smart.)

I myself coached a player who belongs in that class, Isiah Thomas, who helped lead the Detroit Pistons to two consecutive NBA crowns. Isiah is not tall—he's just over six feet—but he could do whatever he wanted with the ball. And what he wanted to do most was lead and win.

All the players I mentioned above and those whom this series will chronicle are tremendously gifted athletes, but for the most part, you can't play professional basketball at all unless you have excellent skills. And few players get to stay on their team unless they are willing to dedicate themselves to improving their talents even more, learning about their opponents, and finding a way to join with their teammates and win.

It's that third element that separates the good player from the superstar, the memorable players from the legends of the game. Superstars know when to take over the game. If the situation calls for a defensive stop, the superstars stand up and do it. If the situation calls for a big shot, they want the ball. They don't want the ball simply because of their own glory or ego. Instead they know—and their teammates know—that they are the ones who can deliver, regardless of the pressure.

The words "legend" and "superstar" are often tossed around without real meaning. Taking a hard look at some of those who truly can be classified as "legends" can provide insight into the things that brought them to that level. All of them developed their legacy over numerous seasons of play, even if certain games will always stand out in the memories of those who saw them. Those games typically featured amazing feats of all-around play. No matter how great the fans thought the superstars, the players were capable yet of surprising them, their opponents, and occasionally even themselves. The desire to win took over, and with their dedication and athletic skills already in place, they were capable of the most astonishing achievements.

CHUCK DALY, now the head coach of the Orlando Magic, guided the Detroit Pistons to two straight NBA championships, in 1989 and 1990. He earned a gold medal as coach of the 1992 U.S. Olympic basketball team—the so-called "Dream Team"—and was inducted into the Pro Basketball Hall of Fame in 1994.

1

"HE LEAVES ME SCRATCHING MY HEAD"

When the referee's whistle signaled time-out late in the heated contest, players from both teams dragged themselves over to their benches. Perspiration drenched their faces, pain shot through their muscles, but the 1988 playoff game in the Los Angeles Forum, pitting the upstart Utah Jazz against the defending champion Lakers, was not over yet. The heavily favored Lakers, led by smooth point guard Earvin "Magic" Johnson, dominating center Kareem Abdul-Jabbar, and sweet-shooter James Worthy, already had captured the first game in this best-of-seven series. A second victory could put the Jazz in a deep hole.

Jazz assistant coach David Fredman remembers thinking that this time-out was crucial for his team. More a war than a friendly athletic challenge, the game had pushed players to their limits, both physically and mentally. The Lakers could let their stars rest by substituting other

The fans go crazy as Utah Jazz point guard John Stockton gets ready to move the ball upcourt.

players, but the Jazz relied on only six men. Two of them, power forward Karl Malone and point guard John Stockton, had played every minute. Could they summon enough willpower to hang in for a few more minutes and pull off an upset, or would the intimidating Lakers sprint to a second consecutive win?

Although he was exhausted, John Stockton never doubted the answer. Taking over the starting point guard position from Rickey Green in this, his fourth professional season with the Jazz, Stockton led the team to a record-high 47 wins in the 1987–1988 regular season. In addition to his 14.7 points per game, Stockton dished out assists to power forward Karl Malone and other teammates at the record pace of 13.8 assists per game. His season total of 1,128 assists shattered the previous mark, set by Detroit Piston guard Isiah Thomas, and made Stockton one of only three men to register more than a thousand assists in one season. His unselfish willingness to hand off the ball to other players rather than score for himself made such an impact on the Jazz that, even though they had had only one winning season before Stockton joined the team, they had not had a losing season since.

Malone, the beneficiary of Stockton's amazing ball-handling skills, claimed, "John is the only point guard in the league who looks to set up his teammates first. He has the ability to make the last-second shot, but he wants to be the guy to set up the last-second shot."

Former teammate Kelly Tripucka added that Stockton's tough defense and his desire to give no less than 100 percent effort each game made him a formidable player. "He's a nuisance, and that's a compliment. He's like a fly that won't go out of the house."

Still, none of this mattered if the Jazz could not reach the championship level. To do this, they had to deal with the Lakers, where they ran into Magic Johnson, a superb guard and a formidable roadblock. Until Stockton wrenched the assist title from his hands in the season just ended, Johnson had owned the category as though it were his by right. Basketball observers believed that Johnson intended to use the playoffs to show that even though Stockton had broken the record for assists, Johnson was still the top point guard. He would show this upstart a thing or two.

Stockton relished the challenge of meeting, in the playoffs, the man considered the best at his position. Many basketball stars would have been delighted with

Stockton goes up for a basket against Magic Johnson during NBA action at the Los Angeles Forum, January 26, 1988. The Lakers won, 111–100.

posting Stockton's regular season numbers, but the Jazz guard believed he had much to learn before he approached Johnson's level. "I have to get to the point where I can do it like Magic does. That means penetrating, scoring more, taking over on offense once in a while, increasing the range on the outside shot to open things up for the drive."

His work paid dividends. Plagued by a dismal playoff record in recent years, the Jazz took three of four games from the Portland Trail Blazers to advance to play the Lakers, owners of the best record in the league.

Game 1 in the playoff series was such a massacre that some wondered if the Jazz could recover. The Lakers' smothering defense held their opponents to a mere eight first-quarter points; their smooth-flowing offense tallied points as if they were playing in a neighborhood match. The lopsided 110–91 loss so demoralized Utah head coach Frank Layden that he was forced to admit, "I don't think we can beat the Lakers."

This set the scene for Game 2, a much closer contest in which the lead frequently changed hands. Late in the game, with the outcome and possibly the entire series in the balance, the Jazz walked over to their bench to huddle for the time-out. Across the way, Magic, Kareem, and James Worthy realized they held the knockout punch in their hands and shouted encouragement to one another. Lakers fans, sensing victory was imminent, rocked the Forum with their chants and shouts. Jazz assistant coach Fredman examined his players' faces and wondered if they had enough strength left in them to wring out a win.

Suddenly, John Stockton, a man of few words who preferred to let his playing speak for him, looked over at Karl Malone and said in a voice filled with confidence, "Mailman, no getting tired now." The two grinned at each other, then returned to the court. Few people knew it at the time, but the momentum had just shifted in Utah's favor.

Stockton's crisp passes set up teammate Malone's accurate shots and led the Jazz to a 101–97 upset victory. Stockton contributed 19 points and 13 assists in the game; Magic's 10 assists were marred by 8 turnovers. For tonight at least, the master was bested by the newcomer.

The series switched to Utah, tied at one win apiece. Stockton continued his wizardry on his home court, dishing out 12 assists and throwing in 22 points for a 96–89 victory in Game 3. Even Magic could do little to halt Stockton's ball handling. For the first time in his playoff career, Magic sat on the bench for the entire fourth quarter.

After the Lakers won Game 4, Stockton single-handedly kept the Jazz in Game 5 until the end. Each time the Lakers pushed to a lead, Stockton roared downcourt to hit an open man with a pass, sometimes with a gentle lob that dropped softly into the man's hands, other times with a zinger that smacked into his palms. Again playing every minute of the game, Stockton added assist upon assist until, with just under one minute remaining, the Jazz led. Still, Stockton's 23 points, 5 steals, and playoff record-tying 24 assists was not enough to hold back Magic and company, who emerged with a grueling 111–109 win.

Although the Lakers led the series 3–2, Stockton had displayed his immense athletic prowess to a nationwide audience. Praise poured in for the point guard. Frank Layden gushed, "Let me put it this way: He is perfect and he is improving. As a pure point guard, I defy anyone to say there has been anyone better. He is Joe Montana. If you need him to pass it hard, he does it hard. If it needs to be a soft pass, he passes it soft. And his ball handling is so good that he makes us virtually press-proof." An opposing coach stated, "Every time I watch him, he leaves me scratching my head."

Stockton typically ignored the flattery. He has always shied from the spotlight, preferring to let others bask in the glow. In fact, Stockton avoids reading newspaper articles about himself because he fears they might distract him, and he never keeps track of his points and assists. "The only numbers I worry about," explains Stockton, "are the number of wins I have."

He needed two more to complete a series victory and advance to the third round. The Jazz came out running from the opening tip-off and, behind a 26–2 run in the first quarter, easily defeated the Lakers 108–80. Stockton's 14 points, 17 assists, and 3 steals meant nothing unless his team could get by the defending champions

It's guard against guard as Stockton fouls Magic Johnson in the first period of a game with the Lakers, December 2, 1988.

one more time. This would be no easy task, since the series returned to Los Angeles.

Dramatic Game 7—the kind that Magic Johnson loved and in which he always produced big numbers—would be a stepping-stone for one team and the season's end for the other. Hollywood stars were sprinkled among the raucous crowd that poured into the Forum in anticipation of a Laker conquest.

Magic performed as expected. Swirling about the court as if possessed, the 6'9" Laker guard tossed in 23 points and added 16 assists. The 6'2" pesky Stockton outdueled his foe by registering 29 points and 20 assists. Unfortunately for Jazz fans, the Lakers could throw more talent on the floor and, with Abdul-Jabbar and Worthy contributing, the Lakers charged to a 109–98 win.

Los Angeles head coach Pat Riley was delighted to have the Jazz out of the way: "I don't think we're ever going to play a better team in the playoffs." As his team moved on to capture another National Basketball Association title, his words were prophetic. Stockton and the Jazz had been defeated, but they proved to onlookers that they were a contending squad with bright hopes for future seasons.

With national attention focused on the series, Stockton was matched against the game's finest point guard and performed brilliantly. His 115 assists in the seven-game series shattered the old mark of 95, held by Magic Johnson. To the winner go the spoils, and in the spring of 1988, John Stockton's prowess on the basketball court was overshadowed by the Lakers and their magical point guard.

Stockton thought nothing of the acclaim. All he cared about was winning and playing his

hardest. "I don't care if people ever discuss what I did," he said, "but if anyone is ever sitting around the kitchen table talking about my career, I hope they say they enjoyed watching me play. That's good enough."

Fans who followed the 1988 Jazz–Laker playoff series certainly appreciated watching a pure point guard like Stockton in action. Even during a time when Stockton's talent rose to the top, another point guard by the name of Magic Johnson enjoyed the fame. If one knows the story of John Stockton's life, one understands that being overshadowed was no isolated phenomenon. It had happened many times before, reaching back to his high school days.

Stockton prefers to set up his teammates with the ball. But when seconds count, the Jazz can rely on him to sink the winning shot.

2

"ALWAYS DRIBBLING A BASKETBALL"

John Houston Stockton was born on March 26, 1962, in Spokane, Washington, a city of just under 180,000 people. When his parents, Jack and Clementine, brought their new son home for the first time to the neat, white and red-brick house on North Superior Street, they planned to impart the same values they stressed to each of their four children—the importance of family, a love of their Catholic faith, modesty about their accomplishments, and the notion that hard work combined with determination leads to success.

To underscore unity in a world that places enormous stress on the family, Jack and Clementine tried to place everything of value within walking distance of home. If the children wanted to see their father during the day, they only had to walk less than two hundred yards to Jack & Dan's, the popular tavern that John's father owned, a block from Gonzaga University. John

Even in his college playing days, John Stockton brought the crowds to their feet with his stunning display on the basketball court.

attended the same Catholic grade school as his father, the same Catholic high school, and the same Catholic university—all within blocks of North Superior Street.

Besides family closeness, the second constant in John's life was sports. Like many youngsters, the Stockton brothers ran to the playgrounds and fields whenever they could to join in the rough-and-tumble games that neighborhood kids organized. No matter how fierce the games were, they paled in comparison with the contests that erupted in the Stocktons' driveway after Jack put up a basketball hoop. Friends might stroll over for a game or two, but the real battles took place when Steve, one of John's brothers, challenged him to a one-on-one game. Steve, taller and older by four years than John, refused to give his little brother a break. Bodies banged into each other, blood and sweat dripped, but neither boy gave an inch. Often losing out to his big brother, John became intensely competitive and ached to win. Although he now goes up against NBA all-stars, John still contends, "I can think of nobody I'd like to beat more than my brother."

He also learned that he had better be tough if he wanted to go head-to-head with his other brothers or the bigger neighborhood boys. One time, he ran into the house in tears after being knocked around. His father looked at John and refused to show any sympathy. "Maybe you shouldn't play with those boys," he said. "Maybe they're too rough." As Jack expected, John took the words as a challenge and hurried back outside. Moments later, he was embroiled again in another brutal pickup game.

John came by his athletic prowess honestly. His grandfather, Houston Stockton, starred as an all-American halfback on the 1924 Gonzaga University football team, which is remembered as the greatest gridiron squad in the history of the school. Inheriting talent is one thing; knowing what to do with it is another. That was the area in which the young John Stockton showed early on that he excelled. Some might let a skill waste away, but John spent every possible moment on a basketball court or in front of the hoop in his driveway, trying to perfect a pass, get a shot down pat, or learn a defensive trick.

John reminded his father of a mailman because he practiced all the time, "in rain and snow, day and night." If he couldn't find anyone who wanted to play, out onto the driveway he went, tossing in shots and dribbling around imaginary defenders hour after hour. He pretended to be one of his favorite players, Seattle Supersonics guard Gus Williams, or tried to copy an older guard he also idolized, Bob Cousy, the legendary ball handler and playmaker of the world-champion Boston Celtics in their glory years.

Because he lacked height and had difficulty shooting over taller defenders, John focused on sharpening the skills that did not depend on height. He honed his defensive abilities, improved his passing and dribbling, and used his speed to learn how to steal the ball from the opponents.

When he was old enough to play for the St. Aloysius Elementary School basketball team, John continued to practice. His coach used to open the school's gym at 6:00 a.m. every day for those who wanted extra work. John Stockton always showed up, no matter the weather. Sometimes, he and some friends would sneak onto the court at Gonzaga University.

Although he showed talent in basketball, no one thought John would ever go far in the sport because of his small stature. He told family and friends that he intended to be a professional basketball player, but as his father explained, "the only person who thought John would play in the NBA was John."

John entered Gonzaga Preparatory High School standing 5'5" and weighing 90 pounds. Although his ball-handling skills were quite impressive by now, he worried that unless he grew he would be overwhelmed, not only by the bigger opponents he would go up against in high school but also by the massive power forwards and centers who monopolized the college and professional ranks. He wanted so badly to gain inches and pounds that his sister, Stacey, remembers hearing John, in the shower, ask God to help him grow as high as the shower curtain.

At least he had quick feet and unusually large hands, features he used to his advantage. His feet gave him an edge on defense; his hands allowed him to control the ball better than most players and to fire pinpoint passes to teammates.

He continued to grow during his high school years, but major college scouts didn't notice him. His size and youthful looks worked against him. And he was overshadowed by two other high school stars from Spokane—Mark Rypien, from nearby Shadle Park High School, and Ryne Sandberg, from North Central High School. When scouts came to town, these were the two they went to see. Sandberg eventually played professional baseball for the Chicago Cubs. Rypien later quarterbacked the Washington Redskins to a Super Bowl victory.

Stockton refused to abandon his dream of making it to the NBA. Rypien remembers "driv-

ing by his house in high school at ten or eleven o'clock at night, and he was always out on the driveway, dribbling a basketball." In Stockton's junior and senior years, he was named to the All-Greater Spokane team, and he earned Most

Stockton protects the ball as Gonzaga plays against the University of Portland, February 11, 1984.

Valuable Player (MVP) honors in his league during his final year.

While Stockton accumulated honors for his basketball prowess, Rypien received the fame that comes with an all-state career. His name was all over the sports section during the football and basketball seasons. Rypien, who like Stockton played point guard, led his team to the state championship in basketball, where he set a record for assists and was named MVP. Typically, though, when the two guards met head-to-head, the scrappy Stockton took it as a personal challenge to best his more heralded opponent. In one high school game, Stockton dribbled circles around Rypien and scored 42 points.

Even with his heroics, big-time college programs ignored Stockton. Scouts worried that Stockton could not stand up to the bone-crushing play of college forwards and centers. As with other important issues in his life, Stockton received help from nearby, familiar faces. In 1980, Gonzaga University, where his father and grandfather had gone to school, offered Stockton a full scholarship to play basketball. Stockton recalls, "I never consciously thought about going through the 'Gonzaga farm system,' but that's the way it happened."

Gonzaga was not considered a top producer of major-league sports talent. With barely 3,000 students in attendance, it received scant notice in the sports pages. Its most prominent graduate was the crooner and movie star Bing Crosby. The national spotlight rarely, if ever, shone on the small college, so if Stockton were to leap into the NBA, he would somehow have to grab the attention of the scouts.

As always, Stockton relied on actions rather

than words. He hoped that if he continued to play with his usual zeal and to practice with determination, the professional scouts would notice him. In effect, he decided to be himself, and if that was not enough for the NBA, well then, so be it. He still believed that he belonged on the same court with Magic Johnson and Larry Bird, and he was determined to prove it.

Playing for a small school like Gonzaga paid instant dividends for Stockton, who reached six feet and 148 pounds by the time he entered his freshman year. If he had gone to a bigger school, such as UCLA, North Carolina, or Indiana, he would have had to fight for playing time with other, more recognized, athletes, and most likely Stockton would have spent more time on the bench than he wanted. At Gonzaga, especially after his first year, he started most games and played enough to sharpen his skills.

Each year, he gradually improved, averaging 15 points per game in his last three years at the school. Stockton finished a brilliant senior year by leading the West Coast Athletic Conference in scoring with a 20.9 average and capping the assists and steals statistics. These numbers earned him the league's Most Valuable Player award for the 1983–1984 season.

As he did when he was a boy, Stockton attacked basketball with every ounce of effort, whether during a game or on the practice court. When a promising high school prospect from Los Angeles, a guard named Steve Kerr, visited Gonzaga to see if he might want to attend, the university's coaches pitted Kerr one-on-one with Stockton, who proceeded to turn the high school star inside out with his smooth moves, swift feet, and accurate shooting. Not only did Stockton sink easy layups and drill outside jumpers, but he

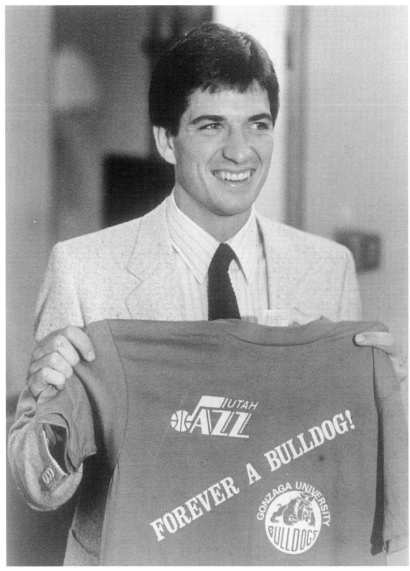

Stockton beams after signing with the Utah Jazz in the summer of 1984. He was their first draft pick.

made mincemeat of Kerr on defense with frequent steals and tenacious play. After the session, the Gonzaga coaches decided against offering Kerr a scholarship. Although Kerr went on to an all-American career at the University of Arizona and later played in the NBA, he walked away from Gonzaga with his tail between his legs.

Professional scouts had not yet spotted Stockton, but other college coaches had seen his wizardry and spread the word. Therefore, in 1984, when coaches were scouring the country for players to try out for the Olympic squad (in those days, professional basketball players were ineligible to compete in the Olympics), they invited Stockton and a few other stars from smaller programs in hopes of finding an unknown talent. Stockton impressed everyone at the Olympic trials with his deft passing and his willingness to outwork any other player. For the first time, Stockton competed with the best in the collegiate world, and he held his own against them.

One day, in the cafeteria, during the trials, Stockton sat down to eat with another hopeful, a man as huge and muscular as Stockton was small. Although neither man could know it at the time, within four years the two not only would become close friends, they would combine to form one of the most potent offensive threats in NBA history. Now, however, John Stockton and Karl Malone simply tried to get better acquainted.

"Out of all those tables," Malone said, "we sat down and started talking. It's kind of amazing, really. Maybe it was fate or something. I thought Stockton was kind of wimpy looking. But I also knew—for him to be there—he had to be a heck of a basketball player. So I introduced myself and we went from there."

Their personal and professional association had to wait, however. Malone was cut in the early going; Stockton lasted until the final 20 players before he was cut. He was bitterly disappointed at not making the final squad; nevertheless, Stockton's superb play drew rave notices from the professional scouts who had assembled to watch this collection of collegiate's finest. In fact, most of the NBA scouts thought that the guard from Gonzaga had outplayed the other point guards. One, in particular, Utah Jazz scout Jack Gardner, planned to tell his bosses of his find when he returned to his office.

3

"THEY ARE SAYING, 'WHO?'"

Jack Gardner faced an uphill struggle to convince his bosses to gamble on this relatively unknown quantity. The Jazz had already started a fine point guard in Rickey Green and hardly needed another, but Gardner argued with conviction that Stockton was a proven winner wherever he played, and he had no doubt that the Gonzaga guard would one day be a superstar. The Jazz owners chose to follow their scout's advice. Since they had to wait until the 16th pick to select their man, they kept Stockton's name quiet, in hopes that no other team had noticed the player.

More than five thousand excited Jazz fans filled the Salt Palace in Salt Lake City, Utah, on draft day, eager to learn the identity of the team's newest player. The 1984 talent pool was probably the richest in history, containing such extraordinary players as North Carolina's Michael

Stockton drives around Nuggets guard Mike Evans (#5) and forward Alex English during first-quarter action in Denver, December 10, 1986.

Jordan, Houston's Hakeem Olajuwon, and Auburn's Charles Barkley. Each turned out to be the best player for the team that drafted him, but Utah knew they would be gone by the time it was the Jazz's turn to pick. Still, the fans could hope. Who knew? Maybe, by some elaborate twist of fate, a big-time player might don a Jazz jersey before the day was over.

As the Utah Jazz was called to announce its choice, noise in the crowded arena stilled to a whisper. "With its pick," proclaimed the commissioner, "the Utah Jazz selects as its first draft pick—John Stockton."

Spectators turned to one another in bewilderment. Instead of the wild cheering that usually occurs with first-round draft picks, the announcement was met with stunned silence. When Jazz television broadcaster Hot Rod Hundley interviewed Stockton by telephone moments later, Stockton heard background noises that sounded like boos.

"Is everybody booing?" he asked Hundley.

"No," answered Hundley, "they're not saying, 'Boo.' They are saying, 'Who?'"

If Stockton experienced an awkward beginning with Jazz fans, he did not let it bother him. Being an underdog and an unknown quantity has its advantages. Stockton vowed to show the fans as well as his opponents what he could do.

Two days after the draft, Stockton asked the Jazz for every game film they could hand over. He spent the interval between the draft and training camp thoroughly studying each film to learn as much about the Jazz offense as he could. He studied every player on the team to pick up on such individual habits as their favorite spot to take outside shots from, whether they could handle hard passes or needed softer lobs, or if they loved to crash the boards. He concentrated on the team's two shooters, Adrian Dantley and Darrell Griffith, to figure out where they liked to receive the ball.

By the time camp opened in the fall of 1984, Stockton had practically memorized the film. Not only did he believe he could orchestrate the Jazz offense but he felt confident that he could produce the basketball at the right spots for each player during games. He may have been smaller and less known than other talents, but Stockton was willing to overcome his deficiencies by outdoing everyone else.

Jazz players and management instantly warmed to the guard from Gonzaga, who put on dazzling displays with razor-sharp passes. Unlike many NBA stars, he did not need to rely upon attention-grabbing passes behind his back or between his legs. Stockton preferred to send the ball straight to his intended recipient, either with a quick pass between bodies or a perfectly placed bounce pass. His determination,

Stockton reaches in on Ralph Sampson's way to the basket in the NBA playoff game against the Houston Rockets, April 21, 1985.

Stockton and Charles Barkley were both in the 1984 talent pool of draft picks. Who knew that years later they would be competing on the court?

intense competitiveness, hatred of losing, and obvious love for the sport endeared him to players and coaches.

Although many NBA members could boast of coming from a huge Division I program, Stockton appreciated what Gonzaga did for him. He claimed that his four years at the university reinforced his willingness to work hard, because he knew he could never slack off if he was to attract the attention of professional scouts. When you play for a smaller institution, he explained, "You know you're an underdog. And when you start to achieve some good results, you still keep that underdog attitude."

Fans quickly sensed that they had found gold when they found Stockton. Not only did he excel in handling the ball but he actually wanted to play for the Jazz. Other top-notch talent made no attempts to hide their disdain for a tiny market like Utah. They wanted the more profitable urban areas like New York or Los Angeles, where more business opportunities and more media coverage

translated into more dollars. Coming from a close-knit family, from a city like Spokane, Stockton felt more at home in the less hectic Salt Lake City community. The town fit comfortably, and that was more important to him than money. When the fans saw this attitude, they had a new hero.

Stockton's first season proved to be one of adjustment. He spent most of the year riding the bench and learning the Jazz's offensive scheme behind starting point guard Rickey Green. Despite this, he still played 18 minutes in each game, averaging 5.6 points per game and setting new club rookie records for assists (415) and steals (109). The team's 41–41 record earned the Jazz a playoff berth, where they upset the Houston Rockets in the first round before losing to the Denver Nuggets in the second.

In the 1985 draft, the Jazz selected a man who would join with Stockton to form one of the most dynamic duos in basketball history. Oddly enough, even though the two blended their talents perfectly and crafted a smooth-running scoring threat, they were opposites off the court. Unlike Stockton, whose family life and childhood years seemed almost idyllic, Karl Malone came from a poor, rural section of Louisiana. Built like a rock, the 6'9", 260-pound Malone played with flair and loved to bring the crowd to its feet with a rousing slam dunk or a wicked block. Malone earned the nickname "The Mailman" because he delivered the "male"—playing a macho, in-your-face game where he used his strength to score many points and pull down lots of rebounds. Opponents learned to be attentive to Malone's presence, mainly to protect their health. In the words of one NBA player, "People tend to get out of Karl's way unless they want their careers to be over."

Malone bonded immediately with Stockton, who although different in many ways, shared his distaste for a flashy lifestyle. "I don't recall exactly why, or what led up to it," Stockton says of their first outing together, "but I remember we went to the zoo."

"With me and John," adds Malone, "what you see is what you get." They both preferred a quieter existence, but even with that similarity, it took time for them to become the close friends they are today. "I always liked John," Malone relates. "But we had to work on getting real close, mainly because we were from such different parts of the world."

No such difficulty existed on the court, where Stockton's ability to move the ball around was just what Malone needed. He was nearly unstoppable when close to the basket, but ball handling was not his forte. He needed someone who could get the ball to him in scoring position, a skill at which Stockton excelled.

Although Stockton's minutes per game increased to 23 in his second season, he was still the backup point guard behind Green. The Jazz compiled a 42–40 record in the regular season, a slight improvement over the year before, but once again they were knocked out of the playoffs with a first-round loss to the Dallas Mavericks.

In a change that showed that the Jazz considered him their guard of the future, Stockton started the next season's first game; he then alternated with Green the rest of the year as starting point guard. He and Malone became more familiar with each other's moves and started to fine-tune their act. In helping guide the Jazz to an improved 44–38 record, Stockton finished in the league's top 10 in both assists (8.2 per game) and steals (2.2 per game).

Once again, the Jazz made a hasty playoff disappearance with another first-round loss. Still, the Jazz coaches liked what they saw in Stockton, who guided the team's offense during the playoffs in place of an injured Rickey Green. His performance in these games convinced them that Stockton was ready to run the offense full-time when the new season started. For the little guard who had always labored in the shadow of other schools or players, the 1987–1988 season could not come soon enough.

4

"HE NEVER TRIES WHAT HE CAN'T DO"

With Stockton as starter, the Jazz finally began to challenge the top-level squads in the NBA. After posting a 47–35 record in the 1987–1988 season, the Jazz captured a Midwest Division title with 51 victories the next year, improved to 55–27 in 1989–1990, and followed with 54 wins in 1990–1991. Observers around the league started considering Utah as one of the NBA's premier powers.

Although the improvement was certainly a team effort, two men carried the bulk of the load —Stockton and Malone. Stockton knew that the team could not rely on him to be its top scorer. If the Jazz were to be successful, Stockton had to bring everyone into the game's flow by hitting them with precise passes when there was an opening—and he was excellent at it. Jerry Sloan, who took over as Jazz head coach in 1988, loved

Stockton's determination shows in every inch of his body. "He has complete control of the game," says Karl Malone. "I don't know what it is he can't do, but he never tries it."

coaching Stockton because he could "pick people out in a congested area."

The Jazz soared to the top ranks in these years mainly because Stockton and Malone so thoroughly fine-tuned their combination that opponents regarded them as the most feared offensive duo in the league. If opponents let up even slightly or were slow after missing a shot, Malone loved to dash downcourt, snare the accurate lead pass from Stockton, and then slam the ball through the hoop, while defenders hopelessly tried to catch up with him.

Sports Illustrated compared their talent to "a figure-skating pairs competition," because Stockton and Malone displayed "the precisely choreographed routines" that were "so beautiful in their simplicity." Seattle SuperSonic veteran Sam Perkins said, "Stockton and Malone set the standard for how a point guard and power forward should play together." Frank Layden, now the team's general manager, didn't mince words: "Seldom in sports do two players make each other better. But these guys, they're like Steve Young and Jerry Rice."

From the start, Malone turned into Stockton's biggest booster. He realized that Stockton would never blow his own horn, so he decided somebody else would have to. "He has complete control of the game," said an admiring Malone. "He's the smartest player I've ever known," because he always seems to know exactly where everybody is on the court and how to get the ball to them. "I don't know what it is he can't do, but he never tries it."

One thing Stockton does try to use in his game is psychology. During one Jazz losing streak, the team warmed up before a game with the Charlotte Hornets. As Malone practiced his moves,

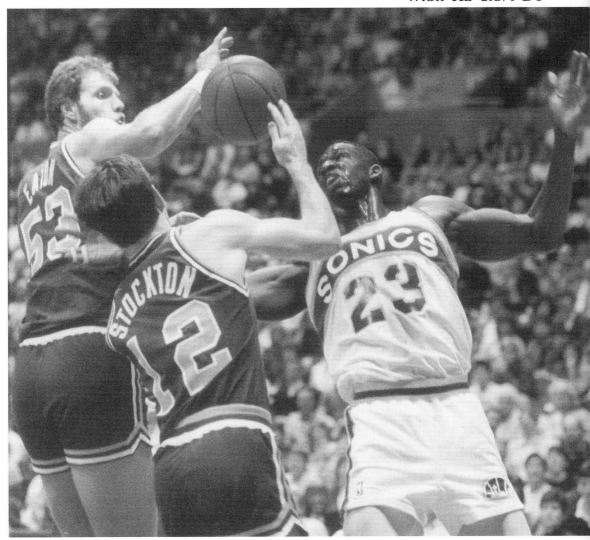

Stockton and teammate Mark Eaton battle for control of the ball with the SuperSonics' Olden Polynice, during action in Seattle on November 29, 1988.

Stockton walked over and told him that a Charlotte sports program on television the night before reported that one of the Hornets said Malone was overrated. Stockton could see Malone's face muscles tighten in anger. He figured the Hornets would be in for a long night. An enraged Malone muscled his way through the Hornets for 52 points to lead the Jazz to victory. Afterward, Malone learned that the clever guard had made up the story to light a fire in his teammate.

Malone claimed that no other guard could come close to touching Stockton's talent. When fans voted Malone into the 1989 All-Star game, he threatened to boycott the game because his friend had not been voted in as point guard. He angrily told reporters that if he did play, he would wear number 12—Stockton's number—on his jersey in his honor. The crisis was averted when the All-Star coaches added Stockton to the team.

Malone was proven right by the game's outcome: he and Stockton put on a show for the entire country. They hit the ground running from the very beginning. Stockton accumulated nine assists in the first quarter alone, with breathtaking passes that set up Malone for a series of crowd-pleasing slam dunks. The furious pace continued for much of the game. By the final buzzer, Malone totaled 28 points and 9 rebounds to earn the game's MVP award. Stockton placed second in the voting, based on his 11 points and 17 assists.

During these four years, Stockton added another honor to his growing reputation—he almost never missed a game. In an exhausting sport that places tremendous physical and mental strain on its players, the Jazz could count on Stockton showing up for every contest, even if he was not feeling well. The only four games he had missed in his entire career occurred in the 1989–1990 season, when he was forced to sit out two games with a sprained ankle and two more because of the flu. Even with the illness, it took an order from Coach Sloan to get him to bed. Stockton appeared at the arena, willing to play, but Sloan sat him down. "When we went to Charlotte the next day," explained Sloan, "we checked him into the hospital."

Stockton's durability throughout his career is even more amazing when one considers that he excels at one of the most physical aspects of the sport—setting screens. A man sets a screen when he plants himself in the way of an on-coming defender so he can spring a teammate into the open. In Stockton's case, this always means allowing a much larger man to bang into him. Not many other NBA stars are as willing to take punishment the way Stockton does, night after night.

"He's the best screen setter on the team," gushed Sloan. "That says it all about him to me." Another coach added that Stockton is "the very best at the underappreciated art of screening."

Watching Stockton sacrifice himself makes Malone grimace. "I worry about John down there getting whacked around by the guys who guard me. John takes them all on." In an effort to help, Malone has let it be known that "anyone who messes with Stockton messes with me," but the scrappy guard has never worried over the matter. In many ways, it is simply an extension of his bruising driveway basketball games from his grade school days.

Stockton and Malone have perfected the play known as the "pick-and-roll." Typically, Malone takes up a position not too far from the basket, and Stockton dribbles past him. Malone's pick rubs out Stockton's defender, and, for a moment, Stockton is uncovered. As either Stockton's or Malone's defender rushes to guard Stockton, Malone rolls to the hoop, and Stockton hits him with a perfect pass. There are numerous variants, of course. Sometimes, Stockton takes the shot if no one comes to guard him quickly enough. Sometimes, Stockton sets the pick and then rolls to the basket, expecting a pass from Malone.

High school kids know how to execute the pick-and-roll and how to defend it. But even though their pro opponents know it is coming, Stockton and Malone run the play so well, there is nothing they can do except give chase, give fouls, and if that doesn't work, give up.

Former point guard Johnny Dawkins says that he wrote off Stockton when he first came into the league. "But I learned that you can't relax for a second with him. He sees everything on the court, and he's aware of everything. You stand

Stockton signs autographs for Japanese basketball fans at a charity function in a Tokyo department store, November 1, 1990.

up for a moment and he's got that quick first step and he's got you on his hip, and he's either laying the ball in the hoop or dishing off to somebody for a basket."

In the 1987–1988 season, Stockton started another streak that lasted for nine consecutive years: leading the league in assists. In his first year as starting point guard, Stockton handily won the league's assist title by averaging 13.8 assists per game, almost two more per game than runner-up Magic Johnson.

Other honors started coming his way, although Stockton has never made individual awards his goal. Between 1987 and 1991, he was placed three times on the All-NBA Second Team and once on the All-NBA Third Team. Twice—in 1989 and 1991—he landed on the NBA All-Defensive Second Team.

Stockton's only disappointment in the first four years that both he and Malone started was the playoff performance of the Jazz. Although they compiled excellent regular season records from 1987 to 1991, the Jazz never advanced beyond the second round after their grueling 1988 series with Los Angeles. High hopes abounded in Salt Lake City that Stockton and Malone could take the Jazz to a championship.

5

"He Makes Dead Meat out of Them"

After posting another fine record of 55–27 during the 1991–1992 season and capturing a Midwest Division title, the Jazz finally advanced beyond the playoff's first two rounds for the first time in franchise history. Series victories against the Los Angeles Clippers and the Seattle Super-Sonics placed them in the Western Conference finals against the Portland Trail Blazers. A third consecutive series win would earn the Jazz a shot at an NBA championship, a goal every player cherishes.

The Jazz split the first four games with the SuperSonics in a string of hard-fought contests. Stockton and Seattle point guard Terry Porter defended each other with such intensity that Porter exclaimed after one of the games, "We're going to be exchanging each other's jerseys if we get any closer." A heartbreaking overtime loss in the fifth game shifted the momentum to Port-

Stockton was picked for the 1992 Olympics, as well as the 1996 Olympics in Atlanta. Here he urges on his teammates in the 1996 gold medal competition.

land, which wrapped up the series with a victory in the sixth game. Stockton performed brilliantly during the playoffs, averaging almost 15 points, 13 assists, and 2 steals per game for 16 contests.

After the playoffs, Stockton joined the other athletes who were selected to participate in the 1992 Summer Olympics, in Barcelona, Spain. For the first time in the history of the Games, professional athletes were permitted to represent their nations, and a delighted Stockton was asked to play alongside Magic Johnson, Larry Bird, and teammate Karl Malone. Anticipating the excitement all this would create back home in Spokane, his father added a beer garden to the back of his tavern to accommodate the crowds. "It's going to be crazy here during the Olympics," Jack Stockton said.

Controversy arose before the players assembled overseas. Even though Stockton regularly led the league in assists, some fans wondered why he was chosen over Detroit Piston point guard Isiah Thomas, who had recently led the Pistons to two straight NBA championships. Ironically, Stockton had been cut from the 1984 Olympic team, when most observers felt he belonged. Now that he was selected in 1992, Stockton's detractors argued he didn't deserve it.

As usual, Karl Malone rushed to his friend's defense and angrily labeled the criticism of Stockton a "disgrace." He did not stand alone. Famed basketball legend Wilt Chamberlain said that if he were forming a team, his first choice would be Stockton. Typically, Stockton ignored the public furor and concentrated on his basketball. "I don't care what people say about me, and I don't care about individual matchups. I just play."

Spectators in Barcelona loved hosting the world's premier athletes, especially the NBA stars. Not surprisingly, Stockton was again overshadowed by other performers. He and Charles Barkley were walking through downtown Barcelona when a tourist spotted them. The tourist approached and, not recognizing Stockton, asked the Utah player if he would take a picture of him and Barkley.

The 1992 Olympics helped ease any pain Stockton experienced over being cut from the 1984 squad, but it was also a bittersweet time. In an early game against Canada, Michael Jordan accidentally kicked Stockton in the leg and fractured his bone. A frustrated Stockton had to watch most of the Olympics from the bench. The coaches finally relented; after Stockton's persistent badgering, they let him play a few moments in the final games.

The Jazz experienced their usual mixture of success and frustration over the next two seasons. After being knocked out in the first round of the 1992–1993 playoffs, the team rushed to a 53–29 regular season record the next year, and swept through two opponents to advance to the Western Conference finals against the Houston Rockets. Although they played in the conference finals for the second time in three years, the Jazz lost four of the five games

Stockton guards the Detroit Pistons' Isiah Thomas during the 43rd NBA All-Star game in Salt Lake City, February 21, 1993.

to the Rockets and went home for the summer instead of playing for the NBA championship.

Stockton's reputation grew during these seasons. In addition to leading the league in assists both years, he shared the MVP award for the 1993 All-Star game with Karl Malone. Played at his home court in Salt Lake City—the sparkling new Delta Center—the game featured vintage Stockton passes and clutch baskets. Stockton's 15 assists and stellar play in overtime helped seal the victory for his squad. In honor of his fine play during the season, Stockton earned a berth on the All-NBA First Team.

Accolades rolled in for the scrappy guard. In 1994, *Sports Illustrated* asked the league's coaches to pick the best players at each position; Stockton's name was at the top. One coach said, "It's not even close. After him, there's a hole a mile wide." Veteran Jeff Hornacek, who joined the Jazz after a trade from Philadelphia, never fully appreciated what Stockton could do until he played alongside him. "I marvel at his anticipation, like a quarterback. I'll come around, off a pick, and in the split second I'm open, the ball will just be sitting there waiting to be shot."

Stockton performs at such a high level night after night because he has an

West teammates (left to right) Utah Jazz's Karl Malone, San Antonio Spurs' David Robinson, Phoenix Suns' Charles Barkley and Dan Majerle, and Utah Jazz's John Stockton celebrate after a three-point bucket by Barkley in overtime at the NBA All-Star game in Salt Lake City, February 21, 1993. The West won, 135–132.

amazing ability to focus his attention on what he is trying to accomplish. He never lets his opponent bother him, either with play on the court or with words. Some of the league's top players engage in "trash talk"—insulting the man they are guarding or boasting that they will drive around and score on their man. Stockton keeps his mouth shut and plays.

"You can't get him out of his game," explained Atlanta's Steve Smith. "He's not going to get in a shouting match with you, he's not even going to smile at you, he's just going to play. He's just focused, and that's one thing I have to give him credit for. I can't play like that. Nothing bothers him. He's not smiling, he's not mad, he's just all basketball."

When new players enter the league, some take Stockton's mild demeanor as an indication that they can drive on him almost at will. They soon learn how wrong they are. Teammate David Benoit said, "I know a lot of other point guards in the league, especially black guys, have said, 'I can take that little white guy.' And then he makes dead meat out of them."

In keeping with his on-court manner, Stockton avoids publicity off the court as well. He prefers to keep as much privacy as possible for his family, which includes his wife, Nada; daughters Lindsay and Laura; and sons Houston, Michael, and David. Rather than living in a stylish mansion in an exclusive neighborhood, Stockton bought the house next door to his parents, fixed it up during the summer, and moved in with his family. Nada has similar roots; she attended Gonzaga University at the same time as Stockton. Although they maintain a second home in Salt Lake City for use during the season, it's their house on North Superior Street or their cabin on Priest Lake, an hour's drive from Spokane, that the Stocktons flee to in the off-season. There, surrounded by childhood friends and family, they feel most comfortable.

"His family is his first priority," states close friend Jeff Condill. "He became more private when he started a family." Steve, his older brother, adds that John has not allowed stardom to change him in any way. "He never holds anything over your head. When the season's over, he comes home and that's it." Away from the public eye, Stockton cherishes the associations he has formed with his classmates and childhood friends.

Although most NBA teams forbid their players from participating in off-season sports to avoid injuries, Stockton purposely added a clause to his contract to allow him to play in summer basketball and softball leagues with his buddies. He approaches these games no differently from his NBA games: Stockton wants to win. "He takes losing personally," says Condill. "Whatever he plays—Ping-Pong, golf, lawn darts. He holds the Jazz record on the treadmill, and he wants to defend that title every year."

Nada says that her husband carries his intensity with him off the court as well. "He likes being home with us, but even at home you can see how competitive John is. Like when he plays games with the kids, basketball or anything else."

Other top athletic talents eagerly seek endorsement fees and television appearances. Stockton avoids television commercials because they infringe on his privacy. To protect his family and maintain a semblance of normal life, he turns down requests for endorsements, even though it means missing out on thousands of dollars. Early in his career, he made a few commercials, but he was uncomfortable in the spotlight. "I did some local commercials, and people recognized me from that more than my six years of service in the league."

Stockton refrains from participating in more than a handful of public appearances, for charities or product endorsements. In 1990, he turned down a request to appear in a poster along with the other two famous Spokane athletes, Ryne Sandberg and Mark Rypien. When *Sports Illustrated* asked to interview him for a planned article on the three stars, Stockton begged out of that as well.

Stockton does not refuse because he's temperamental or hard to get along with. He simply prefers to keep his family out of the spotlight as much as possible. In the case of the *Sports Illustrated* article, he declined because he wanted to help a friend, a fact that impressed the magazine's writers and editors. "What is Stockton doing while he isn't talking to us? He is helping an old friend, the Gonzaga trainer, build a house."

Co-MVP winners John Stockton and Karl Malone (with his daughter) pose for photos with the All-Star MVP trophy after the West team won the 43rd NBA All-Star game.

6

"OFF-THE-COURT HALL OF FAMER"

The Jazz continued to roll up impressive numbers during the three regular seasons between 1994 and 1997. They notched 60 victories in 1994–1995, and they followed with 55 and a franchise-high 64 wins over the next two years. But, once again, the team fell short of an NBA title. After reaching the 1996 Western Conference finals for the third time in five years, the Jazz fought a bitter series with the Seattle Super-Sonics. Seattle quickly jumped to a lead by taking three of the first four games. Utah stormed back to knot the series at three and force a deciding seventh game. In a heartbreaking loss, however, the Jazz tumbled 90–86 and missed out on participating in the NBA finals by five points.

Although Stockton would love to bring a championship trophy to Utah, he is not obsessive about it. He believes the team performs up to its

John Stockton still boasts a winning smile after 13 seasons in the NBA. He plans to remain with the Utah Jazz until he retires.

talents and abilities and has nothing to be embarrassed about. "We were never the best team. The world would have been shocked if we had won. Anything short of being a champion isn't terrific, but we're not the dogs of the league because we haven't won."

The team may have stumbled in the playoffs, but Stockton's excellence on the court put him among the all-time NBA greats. On February 1, 1995, he dished off to Karl Malone for his 9,922nd career assist and shattered the record set by Magic Johnson. Typically, he downplayed his talent when he told reporters that he did not belong in the same class with such gifted playmakers as Johnson and Oscar Robertson. "Those guys are historical players who did so many things, and I don't fit into that category, quite honestly."

To Karl Malone, however, the event made a deep impression. A reporter later asked Malone what his favorite moment in basketball was, and Malone instantly answered, "Taking the pass from Stockton and making the shot for his all-time assist record."

When Stockton led the league in assists for the 1995–1996 season, it marked the ninth year in a row that he won that category. This feat pushed him past the previous mark of eight, set by Bob Cousy, his boyhood idol. Although Stockton wouldn't boast about his achievements, his opponents weren't shy about praising the point guard. Denver's Mark Jackson, who finally ended Stockton's lengthy reign as assist king in 1996–1997, announced that if any young player wants to become an NBA point guard, he should "emulate what Stockton does. He's a class act, and he's done it year-in and year-out."

Gary Payton, the brash point guard from

Seattle who makes no secret of the fact that he thinks he is better than most point guards, chooses his words carefully when he describes Stockton. Asked to list the weaknesses of each point guard in the league, Payton had no difficulty until he came to Stockton. "He's the best," stated Payton. "I'm still looking for a real weakness in his game. If there's one guy I want to be like, it's Stockton."

Stockton added to his luster on February 20, 1996, when he tallied his 2,311th steal, becoming the league's all-time leader and breaking the mark of former Philadelphia 76er guard Maurice Cheeks. He also continued his consecutive-game streak, a streak that went all the way back to the 1989–1990 season, when he missed the only four games in his entire career. Even though he had just recorded his 13th season in the league, Stockton's continued durability and

Stockton and Jazz owner Larry Miller hug each other after Stockton sets a new NBA steal record in 1996.

quickness amazed onlookers. One coach muttered, "When you get Stockton to turn the ball over, it's almost a badge of honor." His streak was broken, however, when he missed the first 18 games of the 1997–1998 season, recovering from arthroscopic knee surgery.

His peers and his fans indicated their appreciation for Stockton when he was selected to play on the 1996 Olympic team and voted into the 1997 All-Star game. Karl Malone hoped that it meant his close friend was finally receiving the praise he deserved. "It goes to show that his

USA's Dream Team III, 1996: (top row, left to right) David Robinson, Mitch Richmond, Hakeem Olajuwon, Scottie Pippen, Grant Hill, Shaquille O'Neal; (bottom row, left to right) Gary Payton, Karl Malone, Reggie Miller, John Stockton, Anfernee Hardaway, Charles Barkley.

game is appreciated in this league, where nowadays guys want to go between their legs, behind their back a thousand times. In the eleven and one half years I've been with him, I think I've seen him go between his legs probably twice, when he had to."

Stockton brushed off being named to the All-Star game by reminding reporters that "a lot of people get a thousand of those [ballots] and start

punching out holes, so you've got to keep it all in perspective and not get excited about it." But he was angry that Malone had not been chosen as a starter. "If Karl Malone isn't starting and I am, there's something wrong with that."

Stockton and Malone had a rapport from the moment they met. Over the years, their friendship has deepened into a family feeling. They spend much of their free time on the road with each other and, as Malone says, they "don't talk basketball all the time. We talk about other things. Families. Kids. Sometimes, we don't even talk. We just keep each other company."

Stockton is the godfather to Malone's oldest daughter, Kadee Lynn. When Malone visited Stockton's family during one off-season, he felt like he had returned home. "I loved it up there," explained Malone. "I loved the country and I loved John's family. They had a helicopter fishing trip all set up. John's dad and his brother—I love those guys. They're awesome. As different as we are in stature and color and all that, we're all the same."

Stockton agreed. "We've never been good at faking things. Everybody was genuinely taken with Karl."

Malone chuckled when he thought about the fishing trip, because Stockton would not let him keep whatever he caught. "Me, I love to hunt and fish. John, he'd never shoot an animal. Never ever. And on that fishing trip, he made me throw them all back."

The love they share for each other and for their families is rare in today's world. But it proves that in spite of the temptations and pressures that beset star athletes, they still can maintain a life of balance. Teammate Bryon Russell says, "Off the court, they're everyday people. They are very family-oriented. You can't catch them without their kids and their wives. If you ask me, they should be in the off-the-court Hall of Fame, too."

In October 1996, Stockton signed a new, three-year, $15 million contract to finish his career with the Jazz. Again, he placed family and team above money by telling everyone the year before that, instead of declaring free agency and attracting big money from other teams, he intended to remain with the Jazz. Stockton could have earned as much as $10 million more if he had gone on the free-agent market, but there are more important things than money in John Stockton's world.

"I'm not leaving Utah. If that turns around and bites me, then that's the way it goes. I'm staying here. I like it here. This is where I'm comfortable, my family's comfortable, and I love the team and the coaches. It'd be kind of a joke for me to say, 'Yeah, I'm going to check my options.' I'm not. To me that's like lying. For me to say I'd go play somewhere else would be a lie. So why do it?" Besides, he says, "Money is not the only issue to me. You can make a lot of bad decisions based only on money."

Utah Jazz owner Larry Miller was delighted but not surprised that his star point guard wanted to stay in Salt Lake City. "Typically, he put the well-being of the team on a par—if not ahead—of what John Stockton could do for himself. There just aren't a lot of guys like John Stockton around any more. John's commitment to this organization is so strong, so focused and so fair, I get kind of emotional when I think about our relationship. I'm so pleased to see John get what this contract gives him and his family." Miller adds, "Stockton has contributed more to this franchise than numbers alone will ever tell."

Stockton intends to remain with the Jazz until he retires, "so I'll give everything that I can for them until they ask me to quit." Besides his deep loyalty to the team, he would hate the idea of not playing with Karl Malone. "I've never really thought about not playing with Karl. I don't think I'd want to. Our individual talents seem to complement each other, so why kill the goose that lays the golden egg just because you want more attention for yourself?"

Malone is even more assertive about his feelings toward Stockton, who he claims "always tries to go out and make his teammates All-Stars. People ask me what I would be without him, and I don't even want to think about it." Malone is bothered that Stockton has yet to receive the acclaim his feats deserve. "When you talk about great guards in history, his name never comes up. I don't understand that. Some people keep asking, 'What has he done?' My question is: 'What more can he do?'"

In 1997, Stockton and Malone did achieve more when they led their team to the NBA Finals for the first time in franchise history. Although they lost to the Chicago Bulls, 4–2, they look forward to returning to the Finals for a championship soon.

Life after basketball has started to come into view for Stockton now that he has completed his

Greg Foster joins Utah Jazz teammates Karl Malone, Jeff Hornacek, and John Stockton after Stockton's three-pointer at the buzzer to win Game 6 of the Western Conference Finals against the Houston Rockets, May 29, 1997.

13th season in the NBA. Although he is not sure what he may end up doing, his business degree and the contacts he has made in the sport have prepared him well. In any event, he is too busy with basketball to worry about retirement, and says, "I'll cross that bridge when I come to it."

Malone is sure of one thing: No matter what he and Stockton do when their basketball careers are over, they will remain in close touch with each other. He looks forward to a time he can "sit down with Stock when things aren't so hectic—when we can just be people, when we're not in such a hurry. There's no doubt in my mind that I'll talk to him two or three times a month for the rest of our lives."

Until then, Malone plans to continue stalking the NBA courts as the recipient of Stockton's razor-sharp passes, and to remind himself how fortunate he is to be paired with such a special player.

"He's so good, you begin to take him for granted," Malone says. "I've just come to always expect the perfect pass from him, and I get it. And I was thinking not long ago, even *I* don't appreciate him as much as I should."

STATISTICS

YEAR	G	FGM	FGA	PTS	PPG	RPG	BLK	AST	APG	STL
1984–85	82	157	333	458	5.6	1.3	11	415	5.1	109
1985–86	82	228	466	630	7.7	2.2	10	610	7.4	157
1986–87	82	231	463	648	7.9	1.8	14	670	8.2	177
1987–88	82	454	791	1,204	14.7	2.9	16	1,128	13.8	242
1988–89	82	497	923	1,400	17.1	3.0	14	1,118	13.6	263
1989–90	78	472	918	1,345	17.2	2.6	18	1,134	14.5	207
1990–91	82	496	978	1,413	17.2	2.9	16	1,164	14.2	234
1991–92	82	453	939	1,297	15.8	3.3	22	1,126	13.7	244
1992–93	82	437	899	1,239	15.1	2.9	21	987	12.0	199
1993–94	82	458	868	1,236	15.1	3.1	22	1,031	12.6	199
1994–95	82	429	791	1,206	14.7	3.1	22	1,011	12.3	194
1995–96	82	440	818	1,209	14.7	2.8	15	916	11.2	140
1996–97	82	416	759	1,183	14.4	2.8	15	860	10.5	166
Totals	1,062	5,168	9,946	14,468	13.0	2.7	216	12,170	11.0	2,531

G   games
FGM   field goals made
FGA   field goals attempted
PTS   points
PPG   points per game
RPG   rebounds per game
BLK   blocks
AST   assists
APG   assists per game
STL   steals

CHRONOLOGY

1962	Born March 26, Spokane, Washington
1980	Enters Gonzaga University on full basketball scholarship
1984	Earns West Coast Athletic Conference's Most Valuable Player Award; meets Karl Malone during Olympic trials; selected by Utah Jazz as its first draft pick
1987–96	Leads league in assists for nine consecutive years
1989	Plays in NBA All-Star Game
1992	Plays for USA in Summer Olympic Games, Barcelona, Spain
1993	Plays in NBA All-Star Game
1995	Breaks league record with 9,922 career assists, February 1
1996	Breaks league record with 2,311 career steals, February 20; plays for USA in Summer Olympic Games, Atlanta, Georgia; signs three-year, $15 million contract with Utah Jazz
1997	Plays in NBA All-Star Game; leads Jazz to the NBA Finals

FURTHER READING

Aaseng, Nathan. *Sports Great John Stockton.* Springfield, N.J.: Enslow Publishers, Inc., 1995.

Biggane, Brian. "Talkin' Trash." *Palm Beach Post,* February 19, 1993.

Blatt, Howard. *Dream Team III: Quest for the Gold!* New York: Pocket Books, 1996.

"Career Profile: John Stockton." *OnLine,* Stockton Player File, February 19, 1997.

Graham, Judith, editor. *Current Biography Yearbook 1995.* New York: The H. W. Wilson Company, 1995.

"John Stockton." Utah Jazz Public Relations Press Packet.

"John Stockton Answers Your Questions." *Online,* USA Basketball Dream Team *Mailbox,* 1996.

Luhm, Steve. "Stock's New Deal: 3 Years, $15-Million." *The Salt Lake Tribune,* September 17, 1996.

"One on One with Karl Malone." *Online,* All-Star Interactive, February 8, 1997.

Rushin, Steve. "City of Stars." *Sports Illustrated,* July 27, 1992.

Taylor, Phil. "Picked Off." *Sports Illustrated,* May 27, 1996.

ABOUT THE AUTHOR

JOHN F. WUKOVITS is a teacher and writer from Trenton, Michigan, who specializes in history and sports. His work has appeared in more than 25 national publications, including *Hoop* and *Sports History.* His books include biographies of World War II Admiral Clifton Sprague, and, for Chelsea House, Barry Sanders, Vince Lombardi, Jack Nicklaus, and Wyatt Earp. A graduate of the University of Notre Dame, Wukovits is the father of three daughters—Amy, Julie, and Karen.

INDEX